Skribbles by K

Karishma Gomez

Copyright © 2020 Karishma Gomez

All rights reserved.

ISBN: 9798696049908

DEDICATION

For my mum, my anchor, my family.

You inspire me every day.

CONTENTS

	Acknowledgments	i
Part 1	Lockdown Tales	1
Part 2	Nature Trails	11
	Chapter 1 – Sunshine	12
	Chapter 2 – Stormy Seas	20
	Chapter 3 – Starry Skies	30

ACKNOWLEDGMENTS

Writing this book has been an incredible journey and I couldn't have done it without the support of my family and friends.

To my mum, Kamini, thank you for your constant love, support and encouragement. And for always believing in me and reminding me that my reach exceeds my grasp.

To my dear friends, thank you for supporting me, listening to my many ramblings and for spreading the love!

A special thank you goes out to two very dear friends, who were incredibly supportive and patiently reviewed *many* poem snippets I shared over the past year.

To Surangi, thank you for embracing this journey as your own and celebrating each milestone with me. And for being my loudest cheerleader and strongest supporter throughout this journey and always.

To Savithri, thank you for being there throughout this journey (with its many storms) and for continuing to inspire and encourage me to follow my dreams.

And finally, to you, my readers, for joining me on this journey and making my dreams come true. Thank you!

PART 1:
LOCKDOWN TALES

What a year it's been,
For all the world, for once in unity
Where every day was strange and bleak,
Full of fear and uncertainty

The rat race that was part of me,
Slowed down unmeasurably
So, when the deafening silence took hold,
All my lockdown tales I wrote,
Determined that it wouldn't break but mould

Holding on to the hope for better days
When I could finally say,
Once upon those lockdown days…

March 2020

Strange Times

What strange times are these,
A temporary norm
Of staying in to weather the storm
While the world outside is shutting down,
All the big cities, now merely ghost towns

We who once roamed far and near,
Over oceans, deserts and atmospheres
Are now bound within 4 walls,
Looking out into a world we once controlled

What strange times are these,
Where uncertainty prevails
And we're forced to live day to day
Anywhere you go, you're greeted with glares,
And the air is filled with fear and despair

What strange times are these,
A temporary norm
We must stay in to weather this storm
And hopefully once this passes through,
We'll appreciate the world a little bit more.

April – May 2020

Wanderlust

Staying in as the long weekend starts,
While wanderlust radiates from my heart
Nowhere to go but the same circular path...

The world has closed its doors,
A stillness echoes from the Earth below
No crazy adventures ahead,
Just the couch or the bed

So grateful for all the adventures past,
Maybe I'll stroll down some familiar paths
Memory lane, let's have a little dance.

June 2020

Grateful

For the fresh air, we can now breathe
For the sunlight shining through the trees
For the music leaking onto the streets,
For the smiles of strangers passing me

For the coffee, now served in porcelain
For the luxury of dine-in vs take away
Grateful for all the little things that make my day
Grateful that we made it through the first wave.

July 2020

The Other Side

Here we are on the other side,
Recovering from our lockdown lives
Weary from a battle we didn't really fight,
Yet playing defense took all our might

Here we are on the other side,
Has lockdown taught us the meaning of life?
Because everywhere I look, I see faces of glee
Of life's simple pleasures and little mysteries

So, as we explore the other side,
Let's continue to be cautious and not slide
For if lockdown taught us anything,
It's that life can change in a blink!

August 2020

Round Two

What's that I hear?
An old familiar tune,
Trickling through the air
Not again, it's too soon
I hear myself sigh in despair

The music is starting,
We keep on dancing,
Staying within the lines
We took one step forward,
And now it's two steps behind.

Tired and weary,
All eagerly waiting,
For this song to end
Round 1 was exhausting,
Round 2 is just starting,
When can we dance freely again?

September 2020

New Normal

Is this the new normal?
The settled state we wanted?
Because it doesn't feel so settled,
The wounds still raw and haunted

Don't get me wrong,
It's great that life has somewhat started,
But I just assumed, we'd be further along,
And the threat would have departed

I still long for the day,
When masks are just for Halloween,
And quarantine is almost never seen
And although vigilant we must stay,
I still hope for 'normal', one day.

October 2020

One Day

I know this fight is dragging on,
And it's getting harder to stay strong
But one day, if relentless we remain,
We will see this villain slain

And on that day,
We'll pop the champagne
But I hope we remember,
What we learnt from the pain

To be united,
To put our differences aside
But most of all,
To be human, to be kind.

November 2020

Lockdown Life

In the blink of an eye,
Trapped inside
While our screens,
Became our eyes

Staying home to stay alive,
Washing our hands,
While singing our rhymes

No end in sight,
Fear hit the aisles,
Resulting in panic excess buys

Demand exceeds supply,
Rations in sight,
Quantifying numbers,
Became a part of life

How many can we buy?
Will it last the time?
Anticipating the end,
One, two, three months, then?

Such were the days in a lockdown life.

PART 2:
NATURE TRAILS

Part two, comes in chapters three,
With a hope to Inspire and comfort thee,
Just as writing it did for me!
So, here's a little summary

Through sunshine or stormy seas,
Starry skies will set you free,
A reminder to always hope and dream!

CHAPTER 1: SUNSHINE

Golden Rays

There's nothing quite the same,
As seeing your golden rays,
Peeking in through the window pane,
To bring you a little yellow and yay!

Or a walk, wrapped in your embrace
Your touch, so warm it could sustain,
So healing, to melt away the pain,
Of the cold night, before your reign

To rise or set, your beauty is seen,
The colours you weave are made of dreams
A reminder with such a blinding roar,
At its start and end, each day is your show

A reminder to celebrate each day,
A reminder that magic isn't far away
With a quiet hope of more time to borrow,
And try again, when you start the morrow.

Bloom

A flower needs to find the sun,
So, its purpose can be done
We too must find what lies within,
A whisper, a spark, however dim

For once we find what makes us sing,
Life become a magical thing
It's not always something we do,
It could be something we hide from too

So, whatever it is, to yourself be true
And take the risk, so you too can bloom
Anything less would be a sin,
For life must be lived, until it's fin.

Second Act

I once was a dreamer,
Before life taught me otherwise
Life taught me to be cautious,
Life taught me to be wise

But then life surprised me,
And reminded me of the fact,
That dreams do still come true,
And sometimes, you get a second act.

Stupid Little Thing

I thought it came with whistles and bows,
Trumpets sounding, candles aglow
But it happens softly, like the falling snow,
Until suddenly, the white blankets show

It's more than sparks and fireworks,
Of holding hands and traveling the world
It's the habits that you start to share,
The morning coffee in cups a pair
The lazy Sunday pancake mess,
The grocery runs that turn into bliss
The little mundane everyday-ness,
That's what makes it the very best!

Flashback

It was just another day,
Until a trigger took her back,
To a different time, a different knack

And as those old memories flowed,
She was reminded of a dream untold

But throughout this flashback trip,
It was a smile that played on her lips

A reminder for times less than bliss
That healing comes softly,
And looks a little like this.

Stages

Saturday mornings like this...
Waking up early with no alarm,
Making coffee, with the music on

A day to give your nine to five a rest,
A day to relax and reminisce,
Takes her back to times different to this

A time when it meant cartoons and chill,
Toaster pastry in hand, what a thrill
Fast forward a decade or so,
When Saturdays meant recovering from the night before

And here we are, back to the present,
Where Fridays are still but oh so pleasant
But Saturdays are special and always will be,
Because it's the day she roams free.

Three's a Charm

Looking back, I realized,
There's been a constant, through my time
At every stage I did find,
A group of three close to confide

From kindergarten musketeers,
And middle school cliques,
To high school babes,
And crazy-pot chicks!

All through my ages,
Threes been a charm
Filled with different faces,
Each with memories so warm!

CHAPTER 2: STORMY SEAS

Growing Pains

Do you remember the days?
When there were no shades of grey
Right and wrong were clearly paved
No questions, no alternates

But life is funny, don't you know
It forces you to bend your rules
Suddenly the lines that were so clear,
Blur into the atmosphere

Decisions you once couldn't comprehend,
Are made between anxious breaths
Constantly torn between heart and head,
Were all villains once heroes, just trying their best?

Seven Years

Seven years, I knew you
Feels like a lifetime ago
Seven years seems so little,
So little to miss you so.

Iceberg

You stood tall like a mighty ship,
And always kept me safe
Then your iceberg hit, it wrecked our ship
And suddenly, everything changed

We made it through the wreckage,
With a void that will never be filled,
But the knowledge that, sun or rain
You will be with us still.

Heartache

A heartache heavier than the seven seas,
But a smile she wears for all to see

Conversations that once set her free,
Are now full of negativity

The one who once calmed all her storms,
Is now for whom she must remain calm.

Sparks

Just kids, playing with sticks and stones
Igniting sparks, we couldn't control
Fanning the flames, with whispers so bold
Playing with fire, danger untold
For what a wildfire, a simple spark did mould.

I Remember

I remember the days,
When I longed for your embrace
New and yet, such a familiar place
Where the world dissolved,
And time slowed its pace

A home to crumble and renew,
Where my troubles seemed less blue
An escape from the daily grind,
I remember the days,
When you were mine.

Rainbow

You were my rainbow,
You caught me by surprise
You brought hues of colour,
Back into my life
And just like a rainbow that promises gold,
I hoped and I prayed for stories untold

But just like a rainbow that fades away,
You moved on and my world turned grey
Struggling to find colour again,
With no rainbow to brighten my day.

Out of Place

We all long to be needed,
To find our place,
Whether at home,
Work or our social space

We all long to be needed,
To feel we can't be replaced

So, we continue to hold on tight,
To things that aren't always right
Because once we find a fit,
It's hard to loosen our grip

Fearing the new and the chase,
Hoping to never again, feel out of place.

CHAPTER 3: STARRY SKIES

Tomorrow

When the dust settles,
And the clouds clear
Even if only for a moment,
Do you take a breath of fresh air?

Or do you spend the now,
Worrying about the next
All you're doing then,
Is wasting a moment of bliss

For here's a little secret,
Something we often forget
Along with tomorrow's troubles,
Also comes tomorrow's strength.

Don't Stop

When the world turns cold and grey,
And the fight just isn't going your way
When the load gets heavy,
And weighs you down
Don't give up, there's good to come

So, do what you need to do,
Take a minute, stop and breathe
Cry it out if it helps you heal
But don't stop moving, there's miles to go
Don't stop now, you're stronger than you know!

Home

This road called life, may lead you astray,
And sooner or later, you lose your way
You become a stranger to yourself,
A greater loss, I cannot foretell
Because people come and people go,
But within yourself, you will always find home.

Midnight Hours

I've always found peace,
Between the hours of twelve and six
When the World's asleep,
Before the day resets

Lost in the silence of it all,
Except for the clicking of the clock on the wall
When the phone doesn't ring,
And the computer doesn't beep
It's blissful silence, that's mine to keep

Time between what was and what will be,
Time to ponder, time to dream
In these hours, my worries sleep,
Midnight hours, come set me free.

Starry Night

Once upon a starry night,
With the sound of waves crashing nearby
Candle light and your hand in mine,
It was perfection with every chime

Between bouts of small talk here and there,
A bittersweet silence filled the air
So much left unsaid and no time to spare,
But in your eyes, I heard it all there.

Grown-up Fairy Tale

There are no happily ever afters,
Where I come from,
Because 'The end' is just a chapter,
Not life's swan song

So no kissing frogs to find the one,
No three wishes or a genie with a bun
No magic carpet to travel the world,
No dragons, that can be slain with a sword

It's a rollercoaster from day one
It's swinging at life's curveballs, head on
It's not about meant to be
But simply that "we" is better than me

It's choosing each other everyday
That's my grown-up fairytale.

Soulmates

Each night we say our lines,
And sing the words we're dealt
And then we're thrown into an act,
To meet the ones, that make us melt

We may not meet in every scene,
Or dance to every song
But there's comfort knowing,
Somewhere on this stage
Our heart has found a home!

So, we keep going on,
And with each act, we grow
Until we've reached our peak,
And when it's time, we'll know

So, after the last encore,
And final bow is done,
I'll reach out, take your hand
And we'll exit the stage as one.

ABOUT THE AUTHOR

Karishma Gomez has two very different passions in life, one is technology while the other is art and creativity. "Skribbles by K" is her first dive into the latter and it's a dream come true.

She is originally from Colombo, Sri Lanka and currently lives in Sydney, Australia. She feels very grateful to call both countries home.

Printed in Great Britain
by Amazon